Stages 10 to 11

Y3/P4

PUPILS' BOOK

Catherine Baker
and Charlotte Raby

OXFORD
UNIVERSITY PRESS

Great Clarendon Street, Oxford OX2 6DP

Oxford University Press is a department of the University of Oxford. It furthers the University's objective of excellence in research, scholarship, and education by publishing worldwide in

Oxford New York
Auckland Cape Town Dar es Salaam Hong Kong Karachi
Kuala Lumpur Madrid Melbourne Mexico City Nairobi
New Delhi Shanghai Taipei Toronto

With offices in
Argentina Austria Brazil Chile Czech Republic France Greece
Guatemala Hungary Italy Japan Poland Portugal Singapore
South Korea Switzerland Thailand Turkey Ukraine Vietnam

Oxford is a registered trade mark of Oxford University Press in the UK and in certain other countries

Extracts and activities compiled by Catherine Baker

British Library Cataloguing in Publication Data

Data available

ISBN: 978-0-19-846745-8

3 5 7 9 10 8 6 4

Printed in China by Imago

Acknowledgements

The copyright for each extract is held by the Author, unless otherwise stated. Extracts (in order of appearance): 'What Are Plants?' from *The Power of Plants* by Claire Llewellyn, TT Non-Fiction Stage 10; *Dustbin* by Michaela Morgan, TT Fiction Stage 10 More Stories B; 'How to make a torc' from *Roman Britain* by Fiona Macdonald, Oxford Connections; *Captain Comet and the Dog Star* by Jonathan Emmett, TT Fiction Stage 9 More Stories A; *Stupid Trousers* by Susan Gates, adapted by David Calcutt, TT Playscripts Stage 10; *Noisy Neighbours* by Geraldine McCaughrean, TT Fiction Stage 9; 'I Like to Stay Up' from *I Like That Stuff* (Cambridge University Press), © Grace Nichols 1984 reproduced with permission of Curtis Brown Group Ltd; *The Ghost Ship* by Martin Waddell, TT Fiction Stage 10 More Stories B; 'Special Soils' from *How to Make Soil* by Sarah Fleming, TT Non-Fiction Stage 10; *The Masked Cleaning Ladies of Om* by John Coldwell, adapted by David Calcutt, TT Playscripts Stage 10; *Jellyfish Shoes* by Susan Gates, TT Fiction Stage 10 More Stories A; 'Animals That Eat Plants' from *Cutters and Crushers* by Claire Llewellyn, TT Non-Fiction stage 11; 'At the Bottom of the Garden' from *Asana and the Animals* (Walker Books), © Grace Nichols 1993 reproduced with permission from Curtis Brown Group Ltd; 'Squirrel' from *Collected Poems for Children* by Ted Hughes, published by Faber and Faber Ltd; *Dexter's Dinosaurs* by Michaela Morgan, TT Fiction Stage 10 More Stories A; 'Wanted! Expert riders ... orphans preferred' from *Sport is Fun!* by David Clayton, TT Non-Fiction Stage 10; *Blackbones Saves the School* by Alan MacDonald, TT Fiction Stage 11 More Stories A; 'Where Does All The Rubbish Go?' from *What's in the News?* by Louise Spencely, Oxford Connections; 'Silver' by Walter de la Mare, reprinted by permission of the Literary Trustees of Walter de la Mare and the Society of Authors as their representative; *Bertha's Secret Battle* by John Coldwell, adapted by David Calcutt, TT Playscripts Stage 11; 'Ancient Egypt' from *Picture Dictionary of Ancient Egypt* by Fiona Macdonald, TT Non-Fiction Stage 11

The publisher would like to thank the following for permission to reproduce photographs: **p6** Corbis; **p7** OUP; **p12** AKG – London/Erich Lessing; **p28**t Alamy/Hido Kurihara; **p28**m Corbis/Andrew Brown/Ecoscence; **p29**t Alamy/Celestial Panoramas; **p29**b Science Photo Lib/Claude Nuridsany & Marie Perennov; **p30**r Corbis/Ted Spiegel; **p30**l Natural Visions; **p38**br Alamy/Holt Studios; **p38**l Corbis/Uwe Walz; **p38**t Getty/Photographer's Choice; **p39** Getty/Image Bank; **p46** Corbis/Bettmann; **p52**b Rex Features; **p52**t Rex Features/Edward Webb; **p61** Corbis/Yann Arthus-Bertrand; **p62**t AKG Images/Andrea Jemolo; **p62**b Corbis/Bojan Brecelj; **p63**t Corbis/Gianni Dagli Orti; **p63**b AKG Images

Cover artwork by Andy Parker

Illustrations: **p6** Martin Aston and Oxford Designers & Illustrators; **pp9,10** Dee Shulman; **p14** Andy Parker; **p17** Martin Remphry; **pp19, 20** Mike Phillips; **pp22, 23** Sue Heap; **pp25, 26** Scoular Anderson; **p28** Paul B. Davies; **p33** Joseph Sharples; **pp35, 36** John Prater; **p39** Barking Dog; **p41** Anna Hopkins; **pp43, 44** Guy Parker-Rees; **pp48, 49, 50, 57, 58** Doffy Weir; **p53** Richard Morris, Pete Smith@Specsart, David Russell; **p55** Gary Taylor; **p61** Mark Duffin

Although every effort has been made to contact the owners of copyright material, a few have been impossible to trace. However, if they contact the Publisher, correct acknowledgement will be made in future editions.

Design by PDQ Digital Media Solutions Ltd

Paper used in the production of this book is a natural, recyclable product made from wood grown in sustainable forests. The manufacturing process conforms to the environmental regulations of the country of origin.

Note to teachers

The texts in this book are differentiated for use with pupils of different reading abilities.
easiest text, medium text, most difficult text

Contents

Introduction

What is comprehension?

Comprehension is all about understanding what you read. It's no good being able to read all the words, if you don't understand what the writer is trying to say!

Here is a quick guide to the top four comprehension strategies that will help you get the most out of all your reading. Use these, and you'll find it easy to understand what you read – and to answer the questions in this book!

Predicting

- Use what you already know to get the most out of a text – before you read, look at the title and think about what it could mean.
- Authors want you to make predictions about characters and plots, so that you are involved in the story.
- When you read non-fiction, think about what you already know about the topic. Linking this with the information in the text helps you to build a bank of knowledge.
- If you recognise the type of text you are reading, it can help you predict how the text will work. But watch out – sometimes authors like to use our expectations to trick us!

Questioning & clarifying

- Whenever you read a text, keep asking yourself questions about it!
- When you are reading fiction, you can ask questions about what the characters are doing and why, or what's going to happen next.
- You can ask questions about why the author chose particular words, or what message they are trying to give us.

- When you are reading non-fiction, asking lots of questions helps you to understand the text.
- You can look for answers to your questions in the text, and it often helps to use your imagination or your own knowledge too!
- You may want to keep a note of your questions, or talk about them with someone else who has read the text.

Imagining

- As you read, think about the pictures in your head. This could be pictures of the characters in a story, or pictures of a scene from a play or poem, or pictures from a description in a non-fiction text.
- Building up these pictures in your head can help you to understand the text.
- As you read on, you can add to the picture you have of the text. Sometimes you will find that you have to change the picture as you read!
- It may help to draw the pictures you see, or write about them, or even act them out!

Summarising

- When you read, you often have to summarise. This means that you bring together information from different parts of the text and use it all together, to help you work out what the text means.
- You summarise when you try to tell someone quickly what the text is all about, or describe the main message the author wanted to give to readers.
- When you read non-fiction, summarising can help you work out the main point of the text, and how the different parts of the text work together.

From *The Power of Plants* by Claire Llewellyn, TreeTops Non-Fiction Stage 10, pages 6–7.

Predicting

What kind of text is this? What is the author trying to tell you?

What are plants?

Plants are living things. They cannot move around like animals but they are still very much alive. They grow, feed, make new plants and eventually die. A big difference between plants and animals is that plants do not have to search for food to eat: they can make it all by themselves.

Leaves make food for the plant. Without leaves, a plant cannot grow.

Stem sucks up water and carries it to other parts of the plant.

Roots take in water and goodness from the soil.

How plants grow

A plant needs light, water and warmth to grow. The roots, stem and leaves of the plant work together to help it survive.

Plants in action: See how plants grow

Materials

Broad bean seed
Soil
Water

Equipment

Tall glass

Method

- Fill the glass with soil.
- Plant the bean under the soil, near the side of the glass.
- Water the soil lightly and keep it damp.

Day 1

Day 7

Day 21

What Are Plants?

Partner activities

I can ...

- find the features of an instruction text
- make notes about the instruction text features I find

1. With a partner, find the part of this text that is like a set of instructions.
2. What clues did you spot that told you that these were instructions? Together, write down three of the clues.

Questioning & clarifying

Keep asking yourself, 'What would I expect to see in an instruction text?'

Think and write

1. Find two differences between plants and animals that are mentioned in the text.
2. How do roots help a plant to grow?
3. Name three things a plant needs in order to grow.
4. Where does a plant get its food from?
5. What kind of plant is shown in the pictures on page 7?
6. How are the children in the picture on page 6 helping plants to grow?
7. What would you use the tall glass for, if you followed the instructions on page 7?
8. Look at the photos on page 7. How does the broad bean seed change between Day 1 and Day 7?
9. Why do you think the Method on page 7 says you have to plant the bean near the side of the glass?
10. Why do you think the author uses photographs to show how the broad bean seed changed?

From *Dustbin* by Michaela Morgan, TreeTops Fiction
Stage 10 More Stories B, pages 10–13.

Dustbin

Predicting

What might be the problem with having a dog that loves eating?

Dylan's dog, Dustbin, just loves to eat!

As the days passed and the weeks passed and the months passed, Dustbin grew fatter and fatter.

Dylan became more and more worried.

'I think we should take Dustbin to the vet,' said Dylan.

In the end, Mum agreed. So off they went to the vet.

'Hmm …' said the vet. 'I want you to keep a diary of *everything* Dustbin eats for five days. Then come back and show it to me.'

Dylan kept the diary very carefully.

He took it back to the vet.

She had a long look at it and sighed.

This is the diary:

Monday

2 dishes of dog food and 1 bowl of water
6 biscuits (chocolate), 1 chocolate fudge cake (and its box), 1 shoe (black)

Tuesday

2 dishes of dog food and 1 bowl of water
8 biscuits (jammy), 1 birthday cake (and its candles)
1 chair (small)

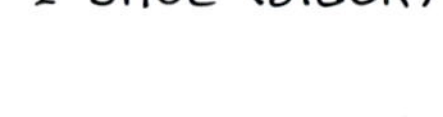

Wednesday

2 dishes of dog food and 1 bowl of water
10 biscuits (custard), 1 shopping bag (and shopping), 1 table leg (wooden)

Thursday

2 dishes of dog food and 1 bowl of water
11 biscuits (with pink icing), 1 pizza (and box)
1 straw hat (crunchy)

Friday

2 dishes of dog food and 1 bowl of water
22 biscuits (mixed), 1 pillow, 1 pair of underpants, 1 wellington boot (chewy),
3 socks (smelly)

Dustbin

Partner activities

I can ...

- **work out how an author uses words to make a text funny**
- **write a short funny text of my own, based on the text I have read**

1. With your partner, write a list of five funny words and phrases from the food diary on page 10.
2. What do you think Dustbin ate on Saturday? Make up your own silly food diary for him. Look at the way Michaela Morgan uses words in brackets to add funny details. Can you do this too?

Imagining

As you read the diary, try to picture Dustbin as he eats some of those silly things!

Think and write

1. Why do you think Dylan's dog is called Dustbin?
2. Why is Dylan worried about Dustbin?
3. What do you think the vet thinks when she reads Dustbin's food diary? Which word in the story gives us a clue about this?
4. Dustbin has a lot of different things to eat and drink, but which two things are the same every day?
5. Why do you think Dustbin eats and drinks these two things every day?
6. Do you think Dustbin likes sweet things or savoury things best? What makes you think this?
7. On which day of the week was it somebody's birthday? How can you tell?
8. On which day of the week did the family order pizza?
9. What do you think is the most surprising thing that Dustbin eats? Why is it the most surprising?
10. What do you think the vet will say when she has read the diary?

Predicting

What type of text do you think this is? How do you know?

From Oxford Connections: *Roman Britain* by Fiona Macdonald Stage 9, page 16.

How to make a torc

Torcs were heavy rings, made of gold, silver or other valuable metals. Celtic people wore them round their necks. The Celts believed torcs had magic powers to protect them from harm. Celtic warriors sometimes fought wearing torcs and body-paint – but nothing else!

You will need:

- tape measure
- pencil and paper
- modelling clay
- modelling tool
- gold or silver paint
- paintbrush

This torc was found in Norfolk

1. Measure the distance round your neck, very loosely. Write down the measurement.
2. Roll out two or three strands of modelling clay (about 10 cm longer than your neck measurement).
3. Twist the strands together carefully.
4. Shape each end of the twisted strands into a loop, a disc or a ball.
5. Add patterns using the modelling tool.
6. Arrange your torc in a curved shape. Do not bring the ends too close together, or you will not be able to put it on.
7. Wait for it to harden.
8. Paint your torc gold or silver, and leave in a warm place to dry.

How To Make a Torc

Partner activities

I can ...

- **read a set of instructions carefully and follow them step by step**
- **evaluate the instructions and think of some ways of improving them**

1. Working with a partner, follow the instructions to make your own torc out of modelling clay. Stop when you get to step 7.
2. How easy was it to follow the instructions? Were any of the instructions unclear, or difficult to follow? Would pictures have helped you understand what to do? Talk about this with your partner and write down two or three ideas to improve the instructions.

Questioning & clarifying

Read right through the text a couple of times before you start to follow the instructions. Try to make sure you know exactly what to do before you start.

Think and write

1. What were Celtic torcs made out of?
2. What did the Celts think was special about their torcs?
3. Why do you think the Celts wore their torcs when they were fighting?
4. When you follow the instructions to make your own torc, why do you need to write down your neck measurement?
5. Why do you need a modelling tool when you are making your own torc?
6. What might happen if the ends of your torc were too close together?
7. What do you think might happen if the ends of your torc were too far apart?
8. Why do you think the author uses numbered points in the instructions?
9. Apart from numbered points, what other features of an instruction text can you find in this text?
10. Draw your own design for a torc. Add patterns and decorations, like those used by the Celts.

From *Captain Comet and the Dog Star* by Jonathan Emmett,
TreeTops Fiction Stage 9 More Stories A, pages 3–6.

Captain Comet and the Dog Star

Predicting

Judging by the picture and the first few lines, do you think this is going to be a scary story?

It was midnight at Stardust Space Station.

Captain Comet, Captain Stella and Spanner the robot had been watching a spooky film about a ghost ship.

'You can come out now, Spanner,' said Captain Comet. 'The film has finished.'

Spanner peeped out from under the lid of a rubbish bin. He looked very scared.

'Are ghost ships real?' he asked.

'Of course not, Spanner,' said Captain Stella, smiling.

Just then, the space scanner beeped.

'It's a spaceship,' said Comet, looking at the scanner screen. 'But it's just drifting.'

Captain Stella tried to talk to the spaceship on the video-link.

'This is Captain Stella of Stardust Space Station. Can you hear me?' she asked.

But there was no reply.

They could see the spaceship on the video screen. It looked old and rusty. The name *'Dog Star'* was painted on its side.

'It looks like a ghost ship!' gasped Spanner.

Captain Comet and the Dog Star

Partner activities

I can ...

- read a text and work out how a character is feeling
- find words and phrases that show how the character is feeling

1. Working with a partner, find a sentence in the text that tells you how Spanner is feeling. What words in the sentence tell you about Spanner's feelings?
2. Look through the rest of the text. Together, make a list of all the words and phrases you can find that show how Spanner is feeling.

Imagining

When you want to find out about a character's feelings, it helps to imagine that you are that character. How would you feel?

Think and write

1. What type of story is this? Find at least three clues that helped you work this out.
2. What is the name of the space station where Spanner, Comet and Stella are?
3. Where was Spanner hiding?
4. Why do you think Spanner wanted to hide?
5. Why does the space scanner beep?
6. What is the name of the spaceship that Spanner, Comet and Stella see?
7. What is unusual about this spaceship? Try to find three things.
8. Why do you think Spanner thinks the spaceship looks like a ghost ship?
9. What kind of character is Spanner, judging from the clues in this text?
10. Write three sentences about what you think will happen next in the story.

From *Stupid Trousers*, adapted by David Calcutt from the story by Susan Gates, TreeTops Playscripts Stage 10, pages 15–18.

Imagining

How would you feel if you had to wear clothes you didn't like to a special event?

Stupid Trousers

Ross has to wear a really stupid pair of trousers to his sister's wedding. They are far too long and he's scared he'll trip up and look silly. He has just been having a row with his brother Lee about this.

Mum Lee! Have you been upsetting your brother again?

Lee No, Mum –

Mum It sounds like it to me.

Lee I haven't, really!

Mum Why is he in such a bad mood, then? Why were the two of you shouting just now?

Lee I wasn't shouting. He was –

Mum It's not fair, you know, Lee. Your sister's getting married tomorrow, and I've got so many things to do. And all you can do is upset your little brother.

Lee But I haven't – !

Mum No more of it, Lee! Do you hear? Or you'll be in big trouble!

She goes.

Lee My little brother! He's the one in the bad mood, and I'm the one who gets the blame! It's just not fair!

Lee goes. The narrators speak.

1st Narrator And off he goes, in a bad mood –

2nd Narrator Because his little brother's in a bad mood.

1st Narrator Because he doesn't want to wear those stupid trousers.

2nd Narrator But if they'd both stayed –

1st Narrator If they'd stayed just a little bit longer –

2nd Narrator They'd have seen that Kerry had solved the problem.

Kerry enters with the trousers.

They are shorter now.

Kerry There. A little bit cut off the bottom of the trousers, a needle and thread to sew them up again, and they're good as new.

She holds up the trousers.

Kerry Just right. They'll fit him now.

She puts the trousers on the chair.

I'll leave them there for him. It'll be a nice surprise when he finds them in the morning.

She goes.

Stupid Trousers

Partner activities

I can ...

- work out why characters are feeling the way they do
- use what I know about the characters in a role-play that shows their feelings

1. Read through the text. With your partner, work out why Lee, Ross and Mum are all feeling upset.
2. With your partner, take the parts of Lee and Ross and role-play a row between them. Lee has to tell Ross that he is fed up with being blamed for things unfairly, and Ross has to tell Lee that he doesn't want to wear the stupid trousers.

Predicting

When you do a role-play, it helps to think about what your character is like. This will help you work out what they would say next.

Think and write

1. When is the wedding that the boys are going to?
2. Whose wedding is it?
3. Which of the two boys is older, Ross or Lee?
4. Why do you think Mum is so cross with Lee?
5. Why does Lee say, 'It's just not fair!'?
6. Why does Ross think the trousers he has to wear are stupid?
7. What does Kerry do to try to put the problem right?
8. Why does Kerry put the trousers on the chair?
9. What differences can you see between the way this playscript is written and the way a story is written? Name at least three differences.
10. What do you think Ross will think when he sees the trousers? Will he be pleased, or not?

From *Noisy Neighbours* by Geraldine McCaughrean, TreeTops Fiction Stage 9, pages 3–9.

Predicting

What kind of text do you think this is, judging by the pictures, the title and the first few lines?

Noisy Neighbours

In a grim, grey house in a grim, grey town lived an unhappy man.

It was not his grey house that made Mr Flinch unhappy. It was not that he was poor, because he was not. Mr Flinch was a miser. He never gave away a penny. (He never gave away a smile either.) He was a mean and miserable man.

Mr Flinch was miserable because of his neighbours.

On one side of Mr Flinch's grim, grey house stood a jolly red one. It belonged to Carl Clutch who mended cars.

Carl loved cars – and motorbikes and vans and lorries. Every morning, Mr Flinch woke up to hear hammers banging, spanners clanging and engines revving. The whole street shook with the noise.

On the other side, in a bright blue house, lived a music teacher called Poppy Plink. Each morning, Poppy sat down and played grand tunes on her grand piano. After breakfast, her students started to arrive.

Violins screeched, drums thundered and bassoons bellowed. Mr Flinch shut his window, but the noise still came through the wall. *Brum-brum, tootle-toot, bang*! His whole house shook and shivered.

He put his fingers in his ears.

He rapped on the wall… but his neighbours did not hear.

They were far too happy. They were mending cars and making music, and they loved their work.

Brum-brum, tootle-toot, bang!

Mr Flinch *rap rapped* until he made holes in his wallpaper. It did no good.

Noisy Neighbours

Partner activities

I can ...

- find some good descriptive words in a story
- add some descriptive words of my own, to describe a character

1. This story has lots of descriptive words. With your partner, make a list of the words that describe Mr Flinch.
2. Sometimes the author uses alliteration. (Using words that start with the same letters like 'grim, grey', and 'Poppy Plink'). With your partner, make up two or three sentences to describe either Carl Clutch or Polly Plink. Use lots of good descriptive words, and try to use alliteration!

Imagining

When you are describing someone, try to picture them clearly in your head. What do they look like? How do they behave?

Think and write

1. What is it about Mr Flinch's neighbours that makes him miserable?
2. Do you think it is fair that Mr Flinch gets so upset with his neighbours? Why, or why not?
3. What does the author mean when she says that Mr Flinch is a 'miser'?
4. What is Carl Clutch's job?
5. Why does Carl's job annoy Mr Flinch?
6. What colour is Polly Plink's house?
7. Which instruments does Polly Plink teach people to play?
8. Why don't Mr Flinch's neighbours hear when he raps on the wall?
9. How can you tell that Mr Flinch must have rapped very hard on the wall?
10. How could Mr Flinch solve his problem? What do you think he will do next?

'I Like to Stay Up' by Grace Nichols from Oxford Literacy Web, *The Mighty Ark and Other Poems* Stage 9, pages 26–27.

Predicting

Look at how this text is set out on the page. What can you tell about it before you even start to read it?

I Like to Stay Up

I like to stay up
and listen
when big people talking
jumbie stories

I does feel
so tingly and excited
inside me

But when my mother say,
'Girl, time for bed'

Then is when
I does feel a dread

Then is when
I does jump into me bed

Then is when
I does cover up
from me feet to me head

Then is when
I does wish I didn't listen
to no stupid jumbie story

Then is when
I does wish I did read
me book instead

Grace Nichols

('Jumbie' is a Guyanese word for 'ghost'.)

I Like to Stay Up

Partner activities

I can ...

- work out what a poem is mostly about
- work out what the main character in the poem is feeling, and why

1. With your partner, read the poem out loud. (Take it in turns to read a verse each.)
2. What is the poem about? Together, think of one sentence that sums up the message of the poem.
3. How is the girl in the poem feeling, and why? Find two words or phrases from the poem that tell you about her feelings.

Questioning & clarifying

When you are trying to work out what the poem is about, ask questions about it. What is the author trying to tell you? Why did the author use these particular words?

Think and write

1. What are jumbie stories?
2. Why does the girl in the story like to stay up listening to jumbie stories?
3. How does the girl feel when she has to go to bed?
4. Why do you think the girl feels like this at bedtime?
5. Why do you think the girl wishes she had read her book instead?
6. Why does the girl call the jumbie story 'stupid' at the end of the poem?
7. How many rhyming words can you find in the poem? Make a list of as many as possible.
8. Find two places in this poem where the language doesn't sound like the type of language you normally find in books.
9. Why do you think the author chose to use this kind of language in the poem?
10. Write about a time when you felt a bit like the girl in the poem. You can write about something that really happened, or you can make it up if you like.

From *The Ghost Ship* by Martin Waddell, TreeTops Fiction Stage 10 More Stories B, pages 14–19.

Imagining

What do you think would happen if you suddenly saw a ghost ship in your school playground?

Everyone had to wait until break time to see the ghost ship. They rushed out of class and into the playground.

'There it is!' Ernie shouted, pointing at the ghost ship.

Everyone took a good look. They saw the bins and the fence, but they couldn't see any ship.

'*We* can't see it,' said Louie.

'But there IS a ghost ship!' Ernie said, looking at it, and *through* it, both at the same time. The ghost ship was see-through and fuzzy.

'There's no ghost ship here!' said Louie.

The ghost seagull flew down and landed on Louie's head.

'A ghost seagull just landed on your head!' Ernie told Louie.

'Oh no it didn't!' said Louie, who couldn't see it, or feel it.

'OH YES IT DID!' Ernie shouted.

'OH NO IT DIDN'T!' roared everyone else.

They laughed at Ernie for making up stories about ghost seagulls and ships. Then they ran off to play.

Along came Jade, the smallest and cleverest girl in Class Four. 'What's that ghost ship doing here?' she asked Ernie.

'You can see it too!' Ernie gasped.

'Of course I can,' said Jade.

'No one else can, but me and Mrs Wiggins,' Ernie said. 'It's Captain Pegleg's ship and he's doomed to sail the sea forever, until he finds his lost treasure. He thinks he left it around here.'

'We could help him to find it,' said little Jade.

'How?' Ernie asked.

'My dad has books about treasure hunting,' said Jade. 'We'll look in his books and find out what to do.'

'Ghost treasure hunt starts right now!' shouted Ernie.

'Ghost treasure hunt starts when we've looked at Dad's books!' said Jade.

The bell went for the start of lessons.

'After school!' Jade told him. 'After school, and no mucking about!'

The Ghost Ship

Partner activities

I can ...

- use my imagination and clues in the story to work out how a character felt
- use role-play to show a character's feelings

1. Read the story, and talk about how Ernie felt at each stage. For example, how did he feel when he rushed outside with the others? When he found out the others couldn't see the ghost ship? When he found out that Jade could see it?
2. With your partner, take the roles of Ernie and his mum or dad. The person being Ernie has to explain what happened. The person being his mum or dad has to ask questions to find out how Ernie felt.

Imagining

When you are trying to find out how a character felt, imagine yourself as the character – how would you have felt?

Think and write

1. How many people can see the ghost ship, and what are their names?
2. What do the other children in Ernie's class see, when he points to the ghost ship?
3. Do the other children in Ernie's class believe him about the ghost ship? Quote a sentence from the text that tells you what they think.
4. Why doesn't Louie believe it when a ghost seagull lands on his head?
5. Find two ways in which the ghost ship is different from a normal ship.
6. How do you think Ernie feels when Jade says she can see the ghost ship?
7. Who does the ghost ship belong to?
8. Why does Ernie think the ghost ship appeared in the school playground?
9. How does Jade offer to help?
10. What kind of person do you think Jade is? Explain why you think this.

From *How to Make Soil* by Sarah Fleming, TreeTops Non-Fiction Stage 10, pages 20–22.

Questioning & clarifying

Before you start to read, think about what you already know about soil and write some notes.

Special soils

Horse carved over 3000 years ago.

Special soil A: Chalky soil

This hill is made of chalk. The soil is very shallow. This makes it easy to dig up so that you can make patterns in the white rock beneath.

The rock

The rock is made of the skeletons of millions of tiny animals that lived in the sea. When England rose out of the sea, the rock made this hill.

England: Upper Cretaceous Period 80 million years ago.

The soil

This soil is so shallow because water soaks through the chalky rock underneath it. When it rains, all the food in the soil is washed away into the chalk. The soil is too poor to let big plants grow. So…the soil never gets lots of dead plants material to make a deep, rich soil. So…the only things that like to grow on poor, shallow, stoney soils like this are grass and wild flowers.

Special soil B: Peat soil

Peat is a special soil made only from dead plants.

Peat is made when dead plants fall into normal soil that is very wet and cold. It takes ages for the plants to break down because it's so wet and cold. The area becomes a bog. Moss grows over it. When the moss dies, it adds to the slowly breaking-down plant material. These layers make 'blankets' of peat.

It takes 10 years for 1 cm of peat to form.

Sundew plants live in peat bogs. They eat insects to add to the poor diet they get from the food-free peat.

Peat is food-free

There is no food in peat. The boggy water and rain washes it all away. With no food, no microbes live in the peat. With no microbes, things take even longer to break down.

So when things fall into a peat bog – a man for example – they too take a long time to break down. When bodies that are thousands of years old are found in peat, they still have their skin, eyes, brain, stomachs and hair!

Uses for Peat

Dry peat burns well. Traditionally, people living near peat bogs would cut and dry blocks of peat and use it like firewood. This is done much more rarely today.

Gardeners like to grow plants in peat because:

- it holds water very well;
- peat compost doesn't come with pests and diseases because it has no food or microbes in it.

BUT

- food has to be added to peat compost to make plants grow.

Rare plants and animals live on peat bogs. The peat bog has become a rare and special habitat. Unless people stop using peat, this habitat may soon disappear.

Special Soils

Partner activities

I can ...

- make notes about what I already know about a topic
- add to my notes, to show what I have learnt from reading a text

1. With your partner, make some notes to show what you both knew about soil before you read the text. Include your own ideas and your partner's.
2. Together, think about what you have learnt about soil from reading the text. Add some more notes to show all the new things that you know.

Questioning & clarifying

Ask yourself questions as you read! If there's anything you don't understand, look carefully in the text for answers. Talk to your partner about your questions.

Think and write

1. Name one thing that makes chalky soil special.
2. Why is it easy to make patterns in chalky soil?
3. Explain why chalky soil is shallow.
4. Why do you think the author included a photo of a horse carved into the soil?
5. Name one thing that makes peat soil special.
6. How do sundew plants in peat bogs get enough food to grow?
7. What happens to bodies that fall into peat bogs?
8. Name two things peat can be used for.
9. Why might it be a bad thing to use peat compost?
10. Name one difference between chalky soil and peat soil, and one similarity between chalky soil and peat soil.

From *The Masked Cleaning Ladies of Om*, adapted by David Calcutt from the story by John Coldwell, TreeTops Playscripts Stage 10, pages 16–19.

Questioning & clarifying

As you read, think about what kind of play this is – is it funny or serious? Is it realistic or a fantasy? Look for evidence to help you make up your mind.

The Masked Cleaning Ladies of Om

King Harry and Queen Norah have lost their cleaner, so King Harry is doing some tidying up, helped by his daughter Jane, Captain Smith and Captain Jones. Suddenly, Queen Norah bursts in…

Queen Norah What on earth do you think you're doing?

King Harry jumps when he hears Queen Norah.

King Harry My dear! We're just… tidying things up a little –

Queen Norah I can see that! Stop it! Stop it at once! Jane! Captain Jones! Put down those shirts!

Jane and Captain Jones drop the laundry.

Queen Norah Captain Smith! Drop that mop!

Captain Smith lets the mop fall.

Queen Norah And you, King Harry! Take off those rubber gloves immediately!

King Harry But, my dear – !

Queen Norah Do as you're told!

King Harry Yes, dear.

King Harry takes off the gloves.

Queen Norah You should all be ashamed of yourselves. I've never seen anything so shocking in all my life. Sweeping and mopping and tidying up. These are not jobs for a king and his captains! You should be out fighting dragons!

Captain Jones (To Captain Smith) Did she say 'dragons'?

Captain Smith (To Captain Jones) I think so.

Queen Norah Yes, I did. That's what you should be doing. Fighting dragons.

King Harry But we've never seen any dragons, dear.

Queen Norah Have you looked for them?

King Harry No.

Queen Norah There you are, then. You won't find them unless you go looking for them. And that's just what you're going to do.

Captain Jones, Captain Smith, and King Harry all speak together.

All What!

Queen Norah You're going on a quest to find a dragon.

Captain Jones And what do we do when we find one, Your Majesty?

Captain Smith *If* we find one?

Queen Norah Fight it, of course! And while you're about it, you can look out for a cleaner as well. I shall expect to see her here at work when I get back.

The Masked Cleaning Ladies of Om

Partner activities

I can ...

- **work out the characters' feelings**
- **use what I know about the characters' feelings in a role-play**

1. With your partner, choose one of you to be Queen Norah. The other one asks questions to find out what she thinks about King Harry and why she is so upset. Queen Norah replies, using evidence from the text and from her own imagination.
2. Swap over and ask questions to find out what King Harry thinks and how he feels about Queen Norah.

Imagining

When you are playing the part of a character, it helps to imagine them as clearly as you can. What do they look like? How do they sit or stand? What expression is on their face?

Think and write

1. Why is Queen Norah so upset that King Harry is doing housework?
2. Why do you think King Harry jumps when he hears Queen Norah?
3. Find two sentences in the text that suggest that Queen Norah is quite bossy.
4. What are Jane and Captain Jones holding when Queen Norah comes into the room?
5. What job is Captain Smith doing when Queen Norah comes into the room?
6. How do you think Captain Jones, Captain Smith and King Harry feel when Queen Norah tells them they are going to go looking for dragons?
7. What excuse does King Harry give for not fighting dragons?
8. Think of two words to describe King Harry, and two words to describe Queen Norah.
9. What do you think will happen next in this play? Will King Harry find a dragon? Will he find a cleaner? Or will something else happen?

Questioning & clarifying

As you read, think about how Laura's feelings change. How does she feel at the start? How is she feeling by the end of the text?

Laura had some new jelly shoes.

She was really proud of them. They were pink and see-through like raspberry jelly.

She ran down to the beach in them. Wherever she walked, they left little tracks in the sand.

Like this:  

'Look, Scott,' Laura called to her brother. 'My new jelly shoes are leaving stars in the sand.'

Squidge. Laura trod in something slippery. She lifted up her shoe.

'Ughhh!' she said. 'What's that mess?'

'It's only a jellyfish,' said Scott. 'The sea washes them up on the beach.'

'Well, I don't like it,' said Laura. 'It looks like a jelly cow-pat.'

Slosh. The sea washed up some more jellyfish. Pink ones this time. They spread out in pink puddles on the sand.

'Watch out,' said Scott. 'Jellyfish can give you a nasty sting.'

'Yuk!' cried Laura. 'There are loads of them! And, phew, what a pong! I hate them. They'll spoil my new jelly shoes!'

Scott looked at the jellyfish on the sand.

He looked at Laura's new shoes. An idea popped into his head.

'I don't know why you hate jellyfish,' said Scott. 'What do you think your new shoes are made of?'

Laura looked down at her shoes. They were see-through and pink. The jellyfish on the beach were see-through and pink too.

'Don't be silly,' she told Scott. But her voice was shaky.

'I thought you knew,' said Scott. 'Don't you know what happens to all these washed-up jellyfish?'

Laura shook her head.

'I'll tell you what happens,' said Scott, who was good at stories. 'The jelly workers come round. They come round at night with bin bags. And they shovel all the jellyfish into the bags. And they take them away to the Jelly Shoe Factory.'

He went on, 'And they make them into shoes. Just like the ones you've got on. I thought everyone knew that!'

Laura looked down at her new shoes.

'I don't think I like my new shoes any more,' she said.

Then she tore them off.

'Yuk!' she said. 'I don't want pongy jellyfish shoes that sting me!'

Jellyfish Shoes

Partner activities

I can ...

- **work out how the main character's feelings change and why**
- **think of words to describe the characters**

1. With your partner, talk about how Laura is feeling at the start of the text. Why does she feel like that? What happens to make her feelings change? How does she feel by the end of the text?
2. Draw a small circle and put Laura's name in it. With your partner, think of words to describe Laura. Write these words around Laura's name. Then do the same for Scott.

Summarising

When you choose words to describe a character, think about all the clues you get about them in the text – including the pictures.

Think and write

1. What is special about Laura's shoes? Name three things.
2. What slippery thing does Laura tread in?
3. Do you think that Scott is younger or older than Laura? What makes you think this?
4. What do the jellyfish on the beach look like? Try to find two different descriptions of them.
5. How do the jellyfish get on to the beach?
6. Why doesn't Laura like the jellyfish? Find as many reasons as you can.
7. Scott tells Laura that her shoes are made out of jellyfish. Do you think he believes this himself? Find a clue in the text that helps you work this out.
8. How does Scott say the jellyfish get to the Jelly Shoe Factory?
9. Why does Laura decide she doesn't like her shoes any more?
10. What kind of story do you think this is? Realistic, a fantasy, serious, funny, or something else? Explain why you think this.

From *Cutters and Crushers* by Claire Llewellyn, TreeTops Non-Fiction Stage 11, pages 6–7.

Predicting

Before you start to read, what do you think this text will be about? When you've finished reading, think about your prediction. Were you right?

Animals that eat plants

Plants are an important food for many animals. Like all foods, they need to be broken down so that the body can digest them. Soft fruits need just a gentle crushing. Nuts and **grains** have a hard outer case, which can be opened by gnawing or cracking. Grasses, leaves and bark are hard to break down, and need a lot of chewing!

Word stretcher

An animal that feeds on plants is called a **herbivore**.

Case study

The horse

Horses feed mainly on grass. They cut the grass with their sharp, front teeth. These are called the incisors. Then they chew the grass on their blunt, back teeth. These are known as the molars. The molars are flat but covered in ridges. As the horse chews from side to side, the ridges grind the grass into a soggy pulp, which can then be swallowed.

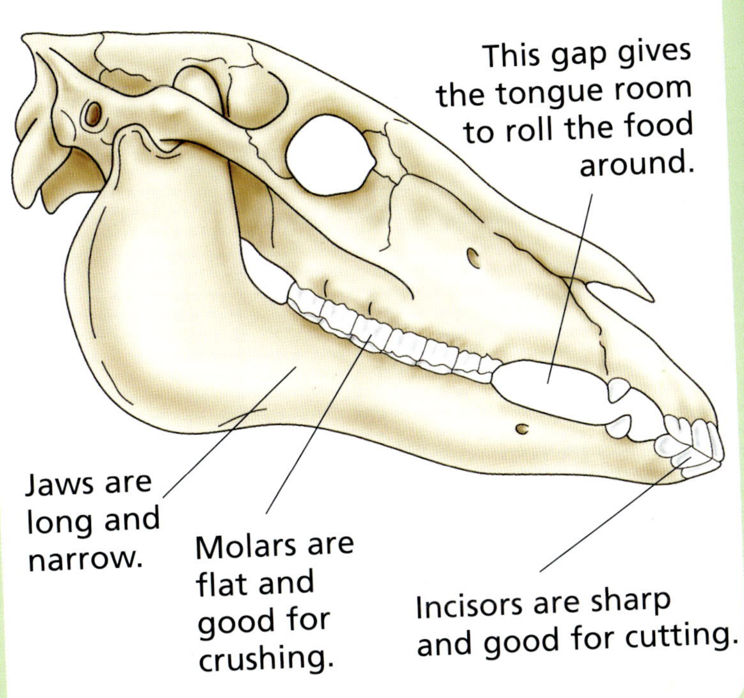

The skull of an animal shows its jaws and teeth. This is the skull of a horse.

What about you?

You eat lots of plant foods, too. Which teeth do you use to bite into an apple? Which teeth mash it to a pulp?

Animals That Eat Plants

Partner activities

I can ...

- read a text and say what it is about
- think of a new title to sum up the text

1. With your partner, talk about what the text is about. Can you think of just one or two sentences to sum up the main point of the text?
2. If you had to think of a new title for this text, what would it be? Discuss this with your partner and agree on a good new title.

Summarising

When you sum up the main point of a text, you need to think about what is the most important information in the text. What is the main thing the author is trying to tell you?

Think and write

1. Why do plants need to be broken down when animals eat them?
2. What do animals use to break plants down when they eat them?
3. Name a type of plant food that is hard to break down.
4. Which are easier to break down – soft fruits or grains?
5. What is the name given to animals that eat plants?
6. Why do you think the author chose to use the photographs on page 38?
7. What do horses use their incisors for?
8. What job do the ridges on a horse's molars do?
9. Why does a horse have to grind grass into a soggy pulp before eating it?
10. What information can you get from the diagram on page 39? Name one thing you can learn from the diagram.

'At the Bottom of the Garden' by Grace Nichols and 'Squirrel' by Ted Hughes
from Oxford Literacy Web, *The Mighty Ark and Other Poems* Stage 10, page 37.

At the Bottom of the Garden

No, it isn't an old football
grown all shrunken and prickly
because it was left out so long
at the bottom of the garden.

It's only Hedgehog
who, when she thinks I'm not looking,
unballs herself to move…
Like bristling black lightning.

Grace Nichols

Questioning & clarifying

While you read these poems, think about what they have in common. How are they similar? How are they different?

Squirrel

With a rocketing rip
Squirrel will zip
Up a tree-bole
As if down a hole.

He jars to a stop
With tingling ears.
He has two gears:
Freeze and top.

Then up again, plucky
As a jockey
Galloping a Race–
–Horse
Into space.

Ted Hughes

'At the Bottom of the Garden' and 'Squirrel'

Partner activities

I can ...

- compare two poems and decide which I like best
- explain my reasons to my partner

1. Read both the poems, and then read them again, out loud. You could read one poem out, and your partner could read the other.
2. Think about which poem you prefer. What do you like best about the poem you chose? Think of at least two reasons why you like it.
3. Talk about your reasons with your partner, and then talk about your partner's reasons for liking their chosen poem.

Imagining

Think about the pictures you see in your head as you read the poems, and how the poems make you feel.

Think and write

1. In 'At the Bottom of the Garden', why does the poet think the hedgehog looks a bit like a football?
2. Does the hedgehog in the poem move quickly or slowly? Quote the words that tell us this.
3. In 'Squirrel', does the squirrel move quickly or slowly? Find two quotes from the poem that tell us this.
4. What is the squirrel climbing, in the poem?
5. What does the poet compare the squirrel to?
6. Do you think this is a good comparison? Why?
7. Find as many rhyming words in 'Squirrel' as you can.
8. Look at the pattern of rhymes in the first verse and in the second verse. How are they different?
9. What do you think the poet means when he says the squirrel 'has two gears: Freeze and top'?
10. Think of at least one way in which these two poems are alike, and one way in which they are different.

From *Dexter's Dinosaurs* by Michaela Morgan, TreeTops Fiction Stage 10 More Stories A, pages 8–13.

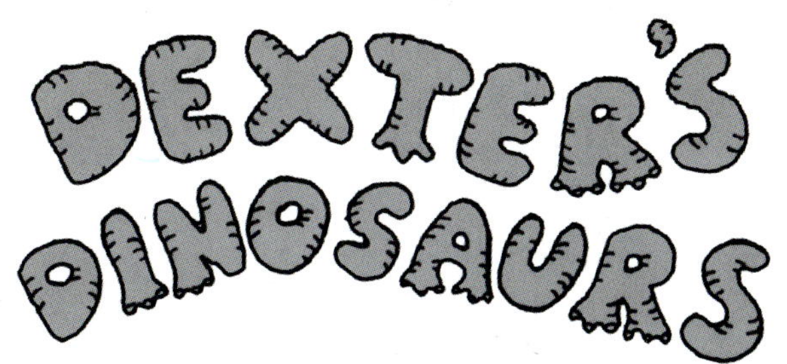

Imagining

Before you read, think about what it would be like to have a dinosaur as a pet. What would be the good things? What would be the bad things?

'What would you like for your birthday, this time?' asked the wizard.

'I'd like to go back in time, please,' said Dexter. 'I want to meet a dinosaur.'

'Back in time!' said the wizard. 'Oh dear me, no. It's much too dangerous back there.

You might be trodden on by a tyrannosaurus.

Or bitten by a brontosaurus.

Or… sat on by a stegosaurus.

Wouldn't you like a nice colouring book instead?'

But Dexter had millions of colouring books already. Most of them were dinosaur colouring books.

'Hmm… I suppose I could bring a dinosaur to you,' said the wizard. 'But I'd need to think up a spell. Let's see…'

'Stop! STOP!' cried Dexter. 'Listen!'

'Aha!' cried the wizard.

'The dinosaur has landed.'

'Ah,' said the wizard, less happily. 'Another one.'

'Oops!' said the wizard. He was beginning to understand what was happening.

'Yes,' said Dexter. 'You've gone too far. You've got carried away. You've asked for too many!'

In the town there was panic. It was raining dinosaurs.

People were shaking and quaking, and running and hiding and SCREAMING.

'Don't worry,' Dexter said. 'Dinosaurs are mostly vegetarians.'

Dexter's Dinosaurs

Partner activities

I can ...

- predict what might happen next in a story
- work with a partner to act it out

1. Read the text. With your partner, decide what you think Dexter and the wizard will do next. Make some notes about it.
2. Act out your ideas about what will happen next. One of you can be Dexter, and one can be the wizard.

Predicting

Don't forget to look for clues in the text. Use what you know about the characters to help you decide what they will do next.

Think and write

1. What does Dexter ask the wizard for as a birthday present?
2. Why doesn't the wizard think Dexter's birthday present wish is a good one?
3. Why doesn't Dexter want a colouring book for his birthday instead?
4. Why does Dexter tell the wizard to stop, when he is saying the spell?
5. What is unusual about the words that show us the noise the dinosaurs make when they land? Why do you think the author and illustrator decided to show the words like this?
6. What do the people in the town think about the dinosaurs?
7. Do you think the people will change their minds when Dexter tells them that dinosaurs are mostly vegetarians?
8. Imagine that the wizard was a friend of yours. What would you ask him to give you for your birthday? Write a paragraph about what you would ask for, and what might happen.

Predicting

Before you read, think about what you already know about how people used horses in the past. Try to think of two or three things you know about this and note them down.

'WANTED! Expert riders... orphans preferred.'

People have been riding horses for thousands of years to fight, hunt and carry messages.

FACT

Pony Express Ad in California newspaper (1860) read: 'Wanted. Young, skinny, wiry fellows. Not over 18. Must be expert riders. Willing to risk death daily. Orphans preferred.'

In America, in 1860, the Pony Express carried messages 2000 miles in 10–20 days.

In Europe, it was mostly royalty and nobles who would ride horses to hunt wild pigs and deer. Only the richest people could afford horses until recently.

In other places, like Russia and Central Asia, ordinary people have ridden horses for 7,000 years.

'WANTED! Expert riders... orphans preferred.'

Partner activities

I can ...

- **read a text and think about what is the most interesting fact**
- **explain to my partner why I thought it was interesting**

1. Read the text and decide what you think is the most interesting thing in the text. It can be in the words or in the picture.
2. Tell your partner which piece of information you thought was most interesting. Explain why you thought this and listen to your partner's ideas.
3. With your partner, decide what was most interesting in the whole text. Together, explain your choice to another pair.

Questioning & clarifying

Keep asking yourself questions as you read the text, e.g. 'I wonder why they did that?'

Think and write

1. Find three reasons why people rode horses in the past.
2. What is the main idea in this text?
3. In 1860, how long did it take the Pony Express to carry a message 2,000 miles?
4. Which country was the Pony Express based in?
5. What do you think of the Pony Express advertisement? Would it persuade you to join the Pony Express? Why, or why not?
6. In Europe, what kinds of people used to use horses for hunting?
7. What kinds of animals were hunted by people riding horses?
8. How long have ordinary people been riding horses in Russia?
9. What do you think the photograph on page 46 shows?
10. Why do you think the author chose this title for the text? Think of another title for this text, that sums up what it is mostly about.

From *Blackbones Saves the School* by Alan MacDonald, TreeTops Fiction Stage 11 More Stories A, pages 4–16.

Blackbones Saves the School

Imagining

As you read, imagine you had a teacher like Captain Blackbones. What would be the good things? What about the bad things?

Suddenly the door flew open. The new teacher strode in. He had a black patch over one eye and a sword at his belt. His beard hung in thick dark curls.

'Ahoy, mates! The name's Blackbones, Captain Blackbones!' he bellowed.

Blackbones sat down on top of his desk. He kicked off his black boots, showing a hole in one sock.

Class 4 gasped as he pulled out his sword – and used it to sharpen a pencil.

He pointed at Yasmin.

'You, matey, what lesson is it?'

'Please Captain, geography.'

Blackbones stroked his beard. 'Ge-og-ruffy. Never heard of it. We'll start with Art.'

Lessons began. They painted a skull and crossbones on the classroom door. With their rulers, they practised sword fighting.

Blackbones winked. 'Now you looks like proper pirates. Let's sail for the sea.'

'The sea's miles away,' said Adrian.

'And Miss Lupin doesn't let us go on trips,' said Yasmin.

Tara had an idea.

'What about the school swimming pool?'

'Just the job! Set sail for the swimming pool!' roared Blackbones. He was enjoying himself. Teaching was far more fun than he'd expected.

Miss Lupin was in the swimming pool with Class 3 when the door burst open.

'Captain Blackbones…!' she began. But it was too late. Blackbones ordered his pirates forward. 'Enemy ahoy!'

Miss Lupin watched in horror as the pirates of Class 4 charged past her. They didn't even stop to change into their swimsuits. They jumped straight into the pool yelling, 'Yo ho ho!'

Class 3 threw rubber rings at the pirates. The pirates threw back plastic floats. Blackbones was everywhere, waving his sword and shouting orders. It was just like the good old days.

All of a sudden Miss Lupin's whistle split the air. Most of Class 3 were up on the diving board. The pirates were about to make them walk the plank.

Blackbones pointed to his class. 'Rattle me cutlass, Miss Lupin. Did I teach 'em well or not?'

Miss Lupin turned to him with a face as black as thunder.

'Get those children down this minute!' she ordered. 'And you, Captain, I want to see you in my office right away.'

Blackbones spent all afternoon in Miss Lupin's office. When he came back he threw his hat on the floor.

'Barnacles!' he muttered.

Tara and Yasmin had waited behind to see him.

'What happened? What did Miss Lupin say?' they asked.

'I've got to go, shipmates,' said Blackbones sadly.

'You mean Miss Lupin has sacked you? After only one day?'

The girls couldn't believe it.

Blackbones sighed. 'I guess I'm no use as a teacher.'

'You're the best teacher we've ever had,' said Yasmin.

Blackbones put on his hat.

'Kind of you to say so, maties. But I've got to go by the end of the week, right after the school fair.'

Tara and Yasmin walked away sadly. If only they hadn't fought Class 3 in the swimming pool. Now Blackbones was going. And they would never get a teacher like him again.

As they passed Miss Lupin's office they heard voices inside. 'We need £10,000 – and that's just to mend the roof!' sighed Miss Lupin.

'This school was started by my Great Aunt Amelia. It's been here two hundred years. Now I'll have to close it down.'

'Maybe the school fair will go well this year?' said Miss Punter, the games teacher.

Miss Lupin shook her head. 'It will take a miracle to make £10,000.'

The two girls were listening outside. Tara grabbed Yasmin's arm. 'That's it!' she said. 'That's how we'll save the captain!'

Next day Tara explained her idea to the rest of Class 4.

All they needed was a way to make £10,000 at the school fair. The school would be saved. And Miss Lupin would be so pleased, she would give Blackbones back his job.

Blackbones Saves the School

Partner activities

I can ...

- think of reasons why characters in a story feel and act as they do
- discuss these reasons with my partner

1. Why do you think the children in Captain Blackbones' class are so keen to keep him as their teacher? Make quick notes of some possible reasons, and then swap ideas with your partner. See how many reasons you can come up with.
2. Why do you think Miss Lupin is less keen on Captain Blackbones? Make notes and discuss this with your partner too.

Questioning & clarifying

Look through the whole text to see how many clues you can find to explain how the children and Miss Lupin feel. Look at what people do as well as what they say.

Think and write

1. What do you think Captain Blackbones did before he was a teacher? Find at least four clues that tell you this.
2. Why can't Captain Blackbones take the class to the sea?
3. Why do you think Miss Lupin is so horrified by what Captain Blackbones and Class 4 do in the swimming pool?
4. Does Captain Blackbones enjoy the session in the swimming pool? How can you tell?
5. What are Class 4 about to do when Miss Lupin blows her whistle?
6. Why does Miss Lupin think she will have to close down the school?
7. How does Miss Lupin feel about closing down the school? Why does she feel like that?
8. What is Tara's idea for saving Captain Blackbones?
9. Find at least one sentence where the author is trying to make you feel sorry for Captain Blackbones.

From Oxford Connections: *What's in the News?*
by Louise Spencely Stage 11, pages 18–19.

Predicting

Before you read, look quickly at the pictures, photos and headings. What do you think this text is mostly about?

Where doe

Growing rubbish problem causes concern

There is increasing concern about the amount of domestic rubbish being produced in the United Kingdom.

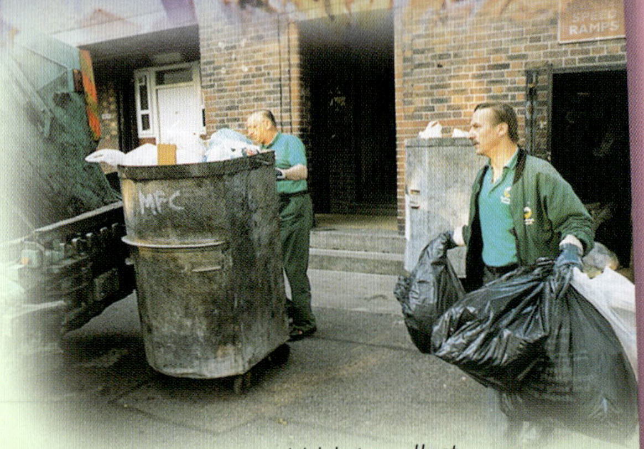

*There would be less rubbish to collect if people **recycled** more things.*

Landfill sites

Most rubbish goes to landfill sites, which are just large holes in the ground, but there is concern about this. There is not much space in current landfill sites and rubbish put in them can take centuries to rot away. People are also worried about landfills poisoning underground water sources, and the sites produce gases which may contribute to **climate change**.

Other ways

We need to find other ways to get rid of our rubbish if we don't want to leave a serious problem for our children and grandchildren to deal with. For instance, shops can use **biodegradable packaging materials**, like cardboard, instead of non-biodegradable plastic or polythene. It would also help to cut down on rubbish if companies sent out less **junk mail**.

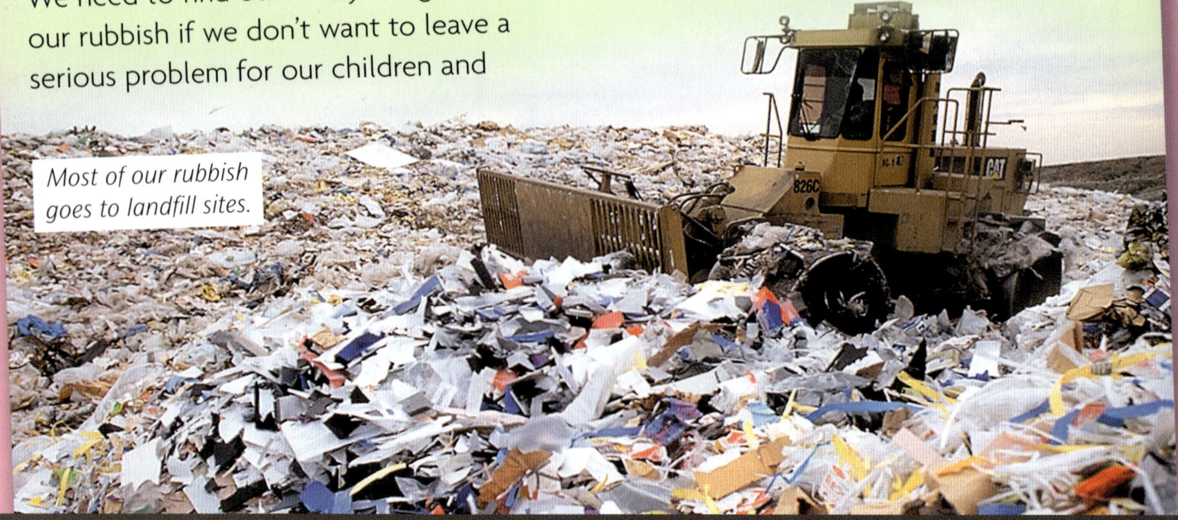

Most of our rubbish goes to landfill sites.

all the rubbish go?

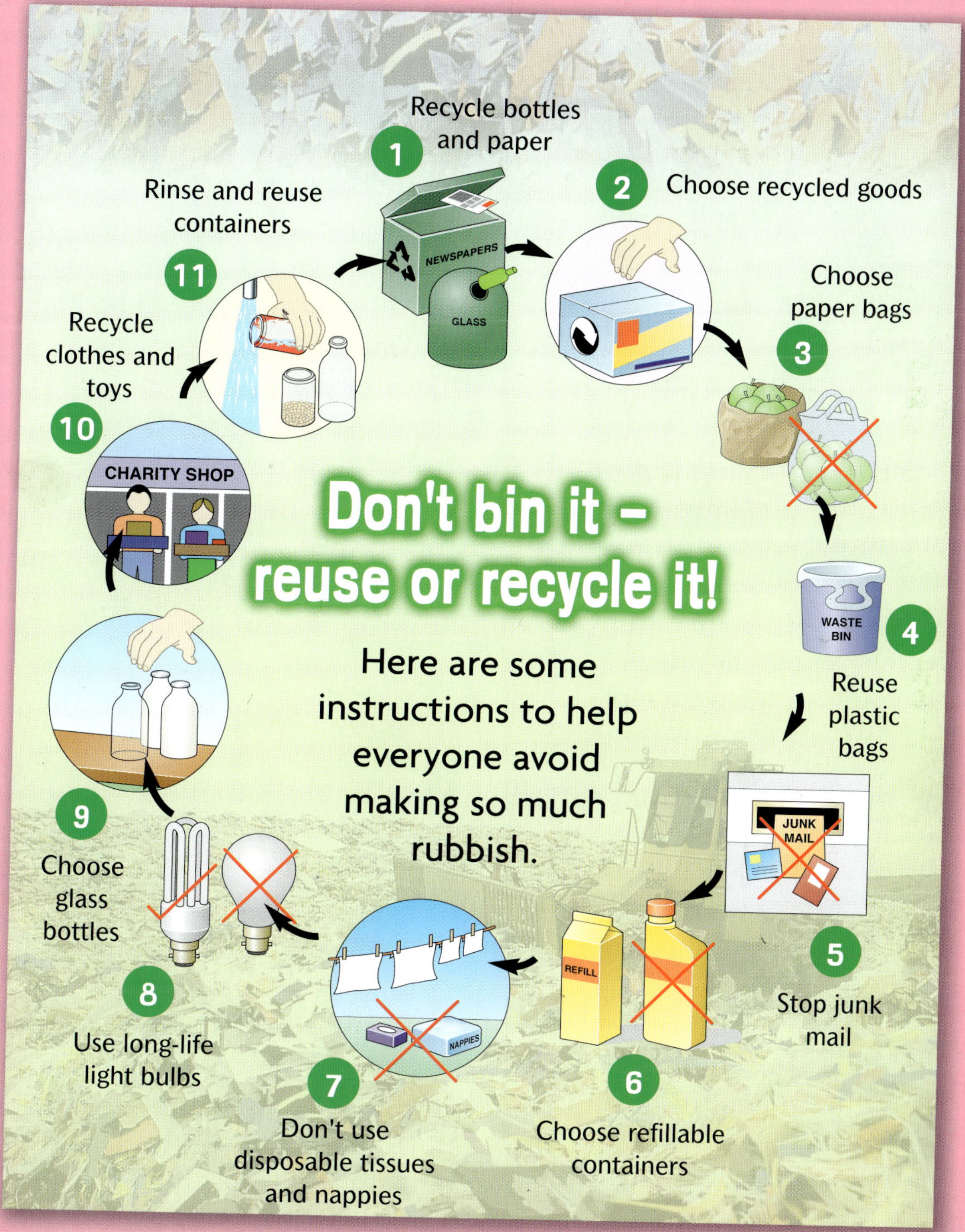

Don't bin it – reuse or recycle it!

Here are some instructions to help everyone avoid making so much rubbish.

1 Recycle bottles and paper

2 Choose recycled goods

3 Choose paper bags

4 Reuse plastic bags

5 Stop junk mail

6 Choose refillable containers

7 Don't use disposable tissues and nappies

8 Use long-life light bulbs

9 Choose glass bottles

10 Recycle clothes and toys

11 Rinse and reuse containers

Where Does All The Rubbish Go?

Partner activities

I can ...

- make up my mind what I think about an issue in a text
- discuss the issue with my partner

1. What message is this text trying to give us about rubbish? Do you agree with what the text is saying? Find one or two parts of the text that you either agree with or don't agree with.
2. Explain to your partner what you think about the issue in the text, and listen and reply to what your partner says. Together, sum up what you both think so that you can tell another pair your views.

Summarising

You need to read and think about the whole text, and look out for key words and phrases that help you understand what the text is saying.

Think and write

1. Where does the text say most rubbish ends up?
2. Find three reasons why people are concerned about rubbish in landfill sites.
3. According to the text, what will happen if we don't find other ways of getting rid of our rubbish?
4. Look at the photo at the bottom of page 52. Why do you think the author chose to use this photo in the text?
5. Why do you think it would help to cut down on rubbish if companies sent out less junk mail?
6. The diagram on page 53 shows a set of instructions. Find at least two ways in which this is like a normal set of instructions, and at least one way in which it isn't.
7. Find one instruction on page 53 that children could follow.
8. Why do you think the author chose to set out the instructions on page 53 in a circle?
9. How do the instructions on page 53 suggest people could reuse plastic bags?

Imagining

Try to picture the scene in your head as you read this poem.

Silver

Slowly, silently, now the moon
Walks the night in her silver shoon;
This way, and that, she peers, and sees
Silver fruit upon silver trees;
One by one the casements catch
Her beams beneath the silvery thatch;
Couched in his kennel, like a log,
With paws of silver sleeps the dog;
From their shadowy cote the white breasts peep
Of doves in a silver-feathered sleep;
A harvest mouse goes scampering by,
With silver claws, and silver eye;
And moveless fish in the water gleam,
By silver reeds in a silver stream.

Walter de la Mare

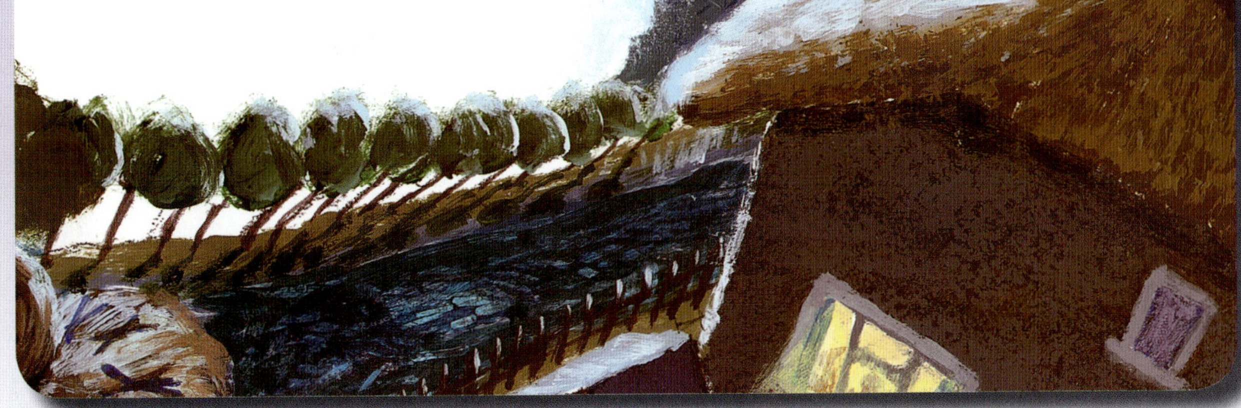

Silver

Partner activities

I can …

- find an example of a description in a poem
- say how a poem makes me feel and why

1. Read the poem and pick your favourite phrase that describes part of the scene.
2. Read out your phrase to your partner and explain why you like it. For example, what picture do you see in your head when you read it? What does it remind you of?
3. With your partner, talk about how the whole poem makes you feel. Do you like it, or not? Try to explain why.

Imagining

Read the poem several times to help you imagine the scene. It may help if you read the poem out loud, or listen to your partner reading it.

Think and write

1. What time of day is it in the poem?
2. The poem says, 'This way, and that, she peers…'. Who is 'she'?
3. Which living creatures are mentioned in the poem?
4. Only one of the creatures is awake and moving – which is it?
5. Is the moon in the poem still or moving? How do you know?
6. Why do you think the poet uses the old-fashioned word 'shoon' instead of 'shoes'?
7. Is the poem set in the country or in the town? How do you know?
8. What do you think the word 'moveless' means?
9. What kind of creature sleeps in a cote?
10. Why do you think the poet chose to call the poem 'Silver'?

From *Bertha's Secret Battle*, adapted by David Calcutt from the story by John Coldwell, TreeTops Playscripts Stage 11, pages 14–17.

Bertha's Secret Battle

Imagining

While you read, think about why Bertha is feeling so upset. How would you feel if you were Bertha?

Bertha and Fiona are twins. They are also wrestlers. When they are wrestling, Fiona always wins ...

Fiona I thought the fight went very well this evening.

Bertha *(Miserably)* Of course it did. It always does.

Fiona It was just like we planned it.

Bertha Of course it was! It always is.

Fiona You're not hurt, are you?

Bertha No. I never am.

Fiona You weren't upset by the flying shoulder-charge?

Bertha No.

Fiona Nor the arm-lock?

Bertha No.

Fiona What's the matter, then?

Bertha There's nothing the matter!

Fiona Yes, there is. You're upset. Why are you upset?

Bertha Do you really want to know?

Fiona Yes.

Bertha All right, then. *(She begins to cry.)* I'm upset because people always cheer you, and they always boo me.

Fiona Of course they do. I'm Fairplay Fiona, and you're Big Bertha the Bone-Cruncher.

Bertha But I'm fed up of being the one they always boo. I want them to cheer me for a change.

Fiona They can't!

Bertha Why not?

Fiona Because you're –

Bertha *(Interrupting Fiona)* I know. I'm Big Bertha the Bone-Cruncher. But I don't have to be all the time.

Fiona What do you mean?

Bertha We could change places. You could be…'Fearsome Fiona'. And I could be…'Big-Hearted Bertha'.

Fiona That's silly. You're so good at being bad.

Bertha I could teach you how to be bad. And you could teach me how to be good.

Fiona No. It wouldn't work. What would my fans think? You're bad and I'm good. That's the way it's always been, and that's the way it always will be!

Fiona goes. Bertha speaks to herself, angrily.

Bertha Oh, yes! That's the way it always is! Fiona's good, and Bertha's bad. It's all right for her, being the good one. She doesn't know what it's like when everybody hates you. And it's about time she did. In fact, if I can think of a plan, this time next week she'll be the bad one, and I'll be the good one. Then they'll boo her, and cheer me.

Bertha goes.

Bertha's Secret Battle

Partner activities

I can ...

- **read a play and work out why the characters feel as they do**
- **role-play being one of the characters**

1. Read the play through with your partner. One of you can read Fiona's words, and one can read Bertha's words.
2. When you have finished reading, take the role of one of the characters and explain to your partner how your character is feeling at the end of the text, and what you think they are going to do next.

Predicting

When you are thinking about what your character might do next, think about what you already know about them from the play. You can also think what you would do if you were them!

Think and write

1. What names do Fiona and Bertha use when they are wrestling?
2. When they are wrestling, do Fiona and Bertha fight for real? Quote a line from the text that tells you this.
3. Name two of the moves that Fiona and Bertha do when they are wrestling.
4. Why is Bertha upset?
5. Why do people always boo Bertha when the twins are wrestling?
6. What idea does Bertha have for changing this?
7. Why do you think Fiona doesn't like Bertha's idea?
8. What does Bertha decide to do, at the end of the text?
9. Do you feel sorry for Bertha? Why, or why not?
10. Will Bertha's plan work, or not? Write a paragraph to sum up what you think will happen next.

From *Picture Dictionary of Ancient Egypt* by Fiona Macdonald, TreeTops Non-Fiction Stage 11, pages 9–11.

Predicting

What kind of text is this? Before you read, look through it quickly and see how many different types of information you can spot.

Gg Hh Ii Jj Kk Ll Mm

Ancient Egypt

desert

Dry, empty, land, where few plants or animals can survive. Egyptians called it 'deshret' (red land). They sent criminals to the desert, to die of hunger and thirst, and buried dead bodies in its salty soil.

Egypt's dry, desert climate has preserved many ancient treasures for us to admire today.

dynasty

Ruling family. Over 30 different dynasties ruled Egypt. The first began to rule in 3100 BC. The last lost power in 30 BC.

Egypt (Ancient)

An ancient kingdom in North Africa, home to a rich civilisation that flourished for over 3,000 years. According to legend, the kingdom of Egypt was created by *Pharaoh* Menes, around 3100 BC. He united two smaller kingdoms, *Upper Egypt* and *Lower Egypt* to form a powerful new state.

Ancient Egypt was larger than the modern country of Egypt, and life there was very different from Egyptian life today.

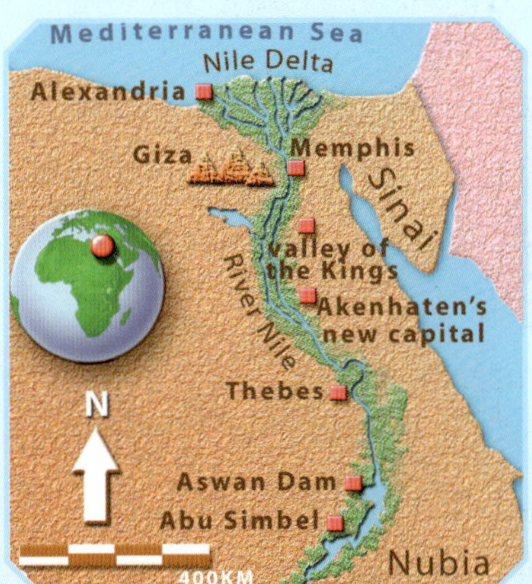

Ancient Egypt was a vast country. It stretched for almost 2,000 km from north to south. It was bordered by desert on the south and west, and by sea on the north and east.

families

Egyptians loved family life. They married young, and hoped to have many children. Men could have several wives, but women only had one husband. Family members had to support each other. Men built houses and grew *food*, women cooked, cleaned, made cloth, raised children and worked as traders. Children helped their parents, and cared for them when they were old.

Egyptian tomb statues often show affectionate families.

farming

Most Egyptians were farmers. They grew grain, beans, lentils, onions, lettuce, melons and cucumber in fields beside the River *Nile*. They planted fig-trees, date-palms and grape-vines, and raised geese, pigs, goats and cattle.

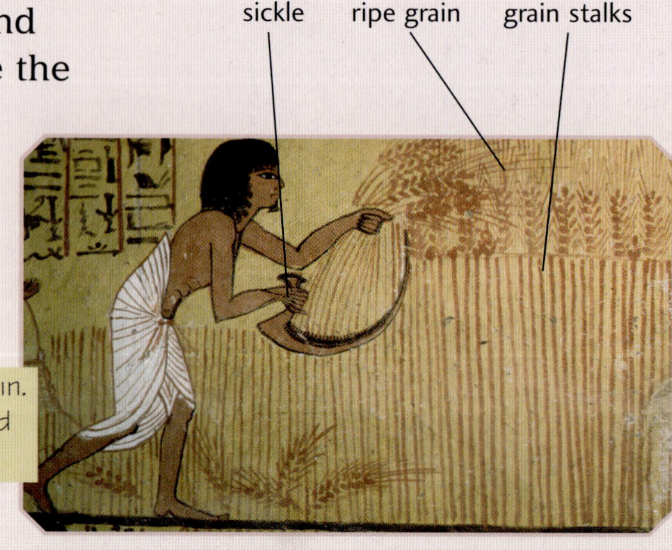

A farmer harvesting grain. He is using a big curved knife called a sickle.

food and drink

Ordinary people ate just one meal a day, of bread, fish and vegetables. They drank thick, cloudy beer, made by mixing bread with water. But rich people enjoyed feasts, with meat, fruit, honey-cakes and wine.

A woman and two male slaves making beer.

Woman with strainer

Barrel of water

Men crushing stale bread

Tubs of beer

funerals

When a *mummy* was ready to be buried, it was placed in a boat-shaped sledge and dragged to a tomb. Women walked alongside, weeping and wailing. *Priests* said prayers and performed ceremonies. Then they closed the tomb.

The most important Egyptian funeral ceremony was called 'opening the mouth'. It was meant to help a dead person's spirit come to live in a mummy.

Ancient Egypt

Partner activities

I can ...

- read a non-fiction text and think about what I already knew about the subject and what I have learnt
- write a short non-fiction text like the ones I have read

1. With your partner, find one piece of information about Ancient Egypt in the text which you already knew, and one piece of information that surprised you. Talk about why you chose this.
2. Together, look in other books about Ancient Egypt, or on the internet. As a pair, write your own information text about Ancient Egypt, like the ones in the text.

Questioning & clarifying

Asking questions as you read the text, and re-reading to find the answers, will help you to understand what you are reading.

Think and write

1. What was the Ancient Egyptian word for desert?
2. What jobs did Ancient Egyptian women do?
3. Name four types of plant that Ancient Egyptian farmers grew.
4. Name one way in which Ancient Egypt was different from modern Egypt.
5. What was one difference between Ancient Egyptian beer and modern beer?
6. Why do you think the author decided to add labels to the photo of a sculpture on page 63?
7. Why did the Ancient Egyptians feel the ceremony of 'opening the mouth' was important?
8. Name a tool that an Ancient Egyptian farmer might have used when harvesting.
9. What happened to Ancient Egyptian criminals who were sent to the desert?
10. Why do you think the author arranged the sections of this text in this order?